ISBN 978-0-656-60485-2
PIBN 11336459

1 MONTH OF
FREE
READING

at

www.ForgottenBooks.com

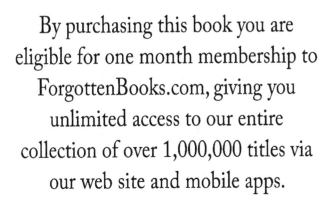

By purchasing this book you are eligible for one month membership to ForgottenBooks.com, giving you unlimited access to our entire collection of over 1,000,000 titles via our web site and mobile apps.

To claim your free month visit:

www.forgottenbooks.com/free1336459

English
Français
Deutsche
Italiano
Español
Português

www.forgottenbooks.com

Mythology Photography **Fiction**
Fishing Christianity **Art** Cooking
Essays Buddhism Freemasonry
Medicine **Biology** Music **Ancient
Egypt** Evolution Carpentry Physics
Dance Geology **Mathematics** Fitness
Shakespeare **Folklore** Yoga Marketing
Confidence Immortality Biographies
Poetry **Psychology** Witchcraft
Electronics Chemistry History **Law**
Accounting **Philosophy** Anthropology
Alchemy Drama Quantum Mechanics
Atheism Sexual Health **Ancient History**
Entrepreneurship Languages Sport
Paleontology Needlework Islam
Metaphysics Investment Archaeology
Parenting Statistics Criminology
Motivational

Historic, Archive Document

Do not assume content reflects c
scientific knowledge, policies, or

الرحيم

ROCK PLANTS AND IRIS

DESCRIPTIVE LIST

CARL STARKER
JENNINGS LODGE
OREGON

Telephones—Oak Grove 195-M
Oregon City 8-F-13

JAMES, KERNS & ABBOTT CO. PORTLAND

INTRODUCTION

OUR gardens are situated on a paved highway ten miles south of Portland, Oregon, on the Oregon City car line, two blocks east of the River road at Hull Avenue station. We have been established since 1915, and have been gradually building up a fine collection of rock plants and iris. Beside the commoner varieties, we have many rare and interesting rock plants, and our collection of tall bearded iris is unusually complete. We have the largest collection of dwarf bearded iris in the west, besides a very large number of Japanese and other beardless iris. Our search for specie iris has been so well rewarded that we can list a number of varieties which are but rarely catalogued.

Order Early. Early orders are suggested to prevent disappointment in case the variety should be sold out. Please write your name and address plainly.

Stock. All orders will be filled with good strong plants that will be reasonably sure to bloom the first season.

Terms. Cash should accompany the order in all cases. No order will be accepted for less than $1.00. Make checks payable to Carl Starker, Jennings Lodge, Oregon.

Postage. We prepay postage and ship promptly.

We do not substitute.

As an inducement for quantity buying, we give six plants of one variety for the price of five. Considering the size of the plants we furnish, our prices are exceptionally low.

Telephones—Oak Grove 195-M
Oregon City 8-F-13

ROCK PLANTS AND PERENNIALS

Realizing that most gardeners want plants that require no pampering, my list includes only a few that are at all difficult to manage. I am continually adding to my stock from the best European sources, and shall by next year be able to list many more new plants of interest. Besides the plants now listed I have limited quantities of many other varieties in my garden. Write me regarding your wants.

If your space permits, by all means use several plants of one kind, rather than one plant each of many kinds. The result will be much more pleasing.

Please order and plant early if possible—early planting is one of the biggest factors of success; besides, stock in some cases is limited.

HARDY PERENNIALS AND ROCK PLANTS
Price of all plants except where noted 25c

Acaena Glauca. Dwarf trailing evergreen foliage of a bluish hue; close spiny heads of flowers. Fine for carpeting.

Aethoenema Grandiflora. Rosy pink flowers. Much like candytuft. May and June. 35c.

Alyssum Saxatile Compactum. Neat bushes, hoary foliage, large heads of golden yellow flowers.

Aconitum Autumnalis. Sept.-Oct. Large blue flowers in racemes. 3-4 ft.

Aconitum Fisheri. Dwarf variety. 2-3 ft. Sept.-Oct. Very useful.

Androsace Languinosa. A trailing plant with silky gray foliage and rose colored flowers. A lovely alpine. 40c.

Anemone St. Brigid. Very early poppy-like flowers of various colors.

Anemone Hupensis. A pretty species from central China with pale mauve flowers from August to late fall. 35c.

Anemone Pulsatilla. Pasque flower. 9-12 in. high. Large flowers, lilac to purple. April and May. An interesting plant for the well drained rockery. 40c.

Aquilegia Flabellata. Nana Alba. Flowers pure white. Plant dwarf. Japan.

Aquilegia Long Spurred Hybrids. Wonderful colors.

Arabis Alpina Flore Plena. Double rock cress. Flowers in dense masses. Splendid for early color.

Arabis Alpina Rosea. Soft rose colored flowers.

Arabis Alpina Variegata. Variegated yellow and green foliage. Very showy.

Arenaria Balearica. A real gem for carpeting a moist, shady spot.

Arenaria Montana. Close tufts of white flowers early in the season.

Armeria Formosa. Neat tufts of dark foliage, round heads of light pink flowers.

Armeria Martima. More dwarf than the preceding, with abundant rose pink flowers.

Aster Alpinus. Large purplish flowers with brilliant yellow centers. Blooms in May.

Aster Alpinus Goliath. Beautiful lilac. 30c.

Aster Bessarabicus. Fine heads of lilac flowers. 12-18.

Aster Climax. Large flowered lavender. One of the showiest.

Aster Cassubicus Grandiflorus. Dwarf dark blue. Fine.

Aster Delavayi. Flowers solitary, large. Delightful shade of lavender blue. Conspicuous jet-black disc. One of the most beautiful of recent introductions. China. 35c.

Aster Mauve Cushion. New hardy Japanese aster. Forms a cushion-like plant 2-3 ft. in diameter and 4-6 ft. high, literally covered with mauve flowers in October.

Aster Perry's White. Remarkably free flowering. Well branched.

Aster St. Egwin. Pleasing rosy pink. Free blooming.

Aubretia Hybrids. Various shades of pink; rose, lavender, and purple. Neat tufts of foliage smothered with flowers in early spring.

Auricula. Handsome primrose-like plants. Foliage covered with whitish powder. Flowers in clusters. Many colors. 35c.

Calmintha. Alpina. Very graceful with rich purple flowers. 6 in.

Campanula Carpatica. Compact tufts of rich blue and white flowers. June to October.

Campanula Glomerata. Large heads of light blue flowers. Very dwarf.

Campanula Moerh Eimei Alba. Similar to Persicifolia, but double white flowers. Very waxy and fine textured.

Campanula Moerh Eimei. Coerulea. Double blue. Same as above.

Campanula Rotundiafolia. Blue Bells of Scotland. Slender branching plants with dainty blue flowers from May to November. Very free flowering.

Campanula Turbinata. Much like rotundifolia, but larger in flower.

Campanula Persicifolia Alba. One of the finest campanulas, with large handsome white flowers in 2-ft. spikes.

Campanula Persicifolia Coerula. Blue. An excellent companion to the white one.

Campanula Persicifolia Backhousei. Very large flowered English hybrid. Colors mixed. 50c.

Campanula Pucilla. Blue. Very dwarf and graceful. 2-4 in. 35c.

Campanula Pucilla Alba. Blooms July and Aug. 35c.

Cheiranthus Allioni. Alpine Wallflower. Covered very early with dazzling orange flowers. 8-10 in. high.

Cheiranthus Cheiri. Wallflower. Wide variety of colors. Some wonderful shades.

Cheiranthus Linifolium. Free flowering lilac. Blooms nearly all summer.

Chrysanthemums. Doubles and singles. Wide variety of colors.

Crucianella Stylosa. Tangled masses of foliage with crowded heads of rose colored flowers.

Delphinium Chinensis. A very pretty species with feathery foliage and intense gentian blue flowers. 12-18 in. June to October.

Delphinium Belladona. Silver blue flowers. Very free flowering. 36-60 in. July to October.

Delphinium, Wrexham and Langdon Strain. Wonderful shades of light and dark blues and lavenders, both singles and doubles. 50c.

Dianthus Alpinus. Very dwarf. Flowers rose to crimson 3-4 in. high, May and June. 35c.

Dianthus Alwoodi. Rose with a dark eye. A very heavy bloomer.

Dianthus Deltoides. Maiden Pinks. Rose colored flowers. June to August. Free flowering 4-6 in.

Dianthus Deltoides Splendens. Carmine rose flowers, dark foliage.

Dianthus **Hedwigi Salmonea Lacinatus.** Extra large fringed, pink.

Dianthus **Lacinatus Alba.** Fringed white. Very sweet scented.

Dianthus **Superbus.** Flowers pale lilac. Very much fringed. Extremely fragrant. July to September.

Digitalis **Buxbaumi.** Yellow Foxglove. Flowers marked with brown.

Digitalis **Monstrosum.** Finest large flowered mixed.

Erigeron **Speciosus.** Beautiful shades of blue. 18 in. June to September.

Erinus Alpinus **Alba.,** Very attractive tufts of green foliage with white flowers. May to July. 3-4 in.

Erinus Alpinus **Carmineus.** Same as above, but with carmine rose flower.

Erysimum **Pumilum.** Very dwarf Alpine species. Large yellow wallflower-like blossoms.

Fragaria **Indica.** Creeping Strawberry. Rapid grower with yellow blossoms and showy red fruits.

Geranium **Grandiflorum.** An extremely large flower. Clear blue. A most unusual plant, and very much admired. The stock is limited. 75c.

Geum **Borisii.** Neat evergreen foliage. Brilliant orange scarlet flowers. Stock limited. 50c.

Geum Lady **Stratheden.** Large double golden yellow flowers. Very fine.

Geum **Mrs. Bradshaw.** Double red. Showy.

Globularia Cordifolia. Metallic blue leaves in winter. Round heads of pretty blue flowers.

Gypsophylla. Paniculata. Small white flowers in great profusion. Useful for bouquets.

Gypsophylla Repens. White flowers, trailer. Good rock plant.

Helleborus **Niger.** Christmas Rose. Blooms all winter. Anemone-like flowers. Tinted like apple blossoms. Very lovely for a sunny corner in winter. Rare. 75c.

Helianthemum Vulgare. Rock Rose. Various shades, white, yellow, pinks, and reds. Flowers like miniature wild roses. Constant bloomer. Doubles and singles. Showy. 25c-50c.

Heuchera **Sanguinea.** Coral Bells. Coral red flowers 12 in. high in loose panicles.

Hypericum **Reptans.** Prostrate evergreen glaucous foliage. Large golden yellow flowers. 35c.

Hypericum. From White River glacier. A charming carpeter with minute bronze foliage and tiny yellow flowers. 35c.

Linaria Alpina. Flowers bluish violet, like small snapdragons. Dwarf.

Leontopodium Alpinum. Edelweiss. A well known Alpine. Small yellow flowers surrounded by star-like heads of leaves clothed with a dense woolly substance. 4-6 in. 35c.

Linum Narbonense. Elegant blue green foliage, graceful arching stems, beautiful circular blue flowers.

Linum Perenne. Intense sky blue flowers.

Lychnis Alpina. Pink flowers, April and May. 3-4 in.

Lychnis Viscaria Flore Pleno. Very double brilliant carmine flowers, April to July. 6-8 in.

Lysimachia **Nummularia.** Pretty flat growing evergreen trailer with yellow flowers.

Mentha **Requieni.** Dense green carpet of fragrant mint foliage. 35c.

Myosotis. Alpine Forgetmenot, dwarf and free flowering.

Nepeta **Mussini.** A fine rock mint for sunny locations. Lovely clouds of soft lavender blue flowers all summer. 12 in. high.

Papaver Orientalis. Various shades of pink and red.

Pentstemon Glaber. Fine evergreen foliage, brilliant tubular, bright blue flowers.

Phlox. Amoena. One of the best for carpeting. 4 in. high, a sheet of bright pink in early spring.

Phlox Canadensis. Neat tufted habit, slender stems with heads of lovely lavender blue flowers.

Phlox Sublata. Mossy Phlox. A charming creeper, covered in very early spring with masses of flowers. Two separate colors, white or rose.

Polemonium Humile. Low slender plant, flowers bell shape, blue, with the odor of grapes.

Polemonium Reptans. One foot or less. Blue flowers.

Polemonium Richardsonii. About 18 in. high. Various shades of blue.

Plumbago Larpentae. Dwarf spreading habit, bronze foliage, deep blue flowers in fall. 6-8 in.

Primula Cashmeriana. Earliest of all, with umbels of rosy lilac to white flowers. 50c.

Primula Japonica. Hybrids. New hybrids of rose, orange and carmine flowers in whorls. 10-14 in. 50c.

Primula Veris. Hardy primrose. Splendid border plant. Our strain includes various shades of blue, buff, orange, red, pink and yellow. We also have cowslips and hose-in-hose types. 15c to 50c.

Pyrethrum Grandiflorum. Daisy-like flowers, white to dark rose, doubles and singles. 18 in.

Sagina. Densely tufted plant, covering the ground like sheet moss, flowers white, studded all over the plant.

Saponaria Calabrica. Brilliant masses of pink flowers in spring.

Saponaria Ocymoides. Lovely pinkish rose blossoms, very free flowering.

Saxifraga Aizoon. A valuable alpine, much tufted, forming dense rosettes, flowers white, 6-10 in.

Saxifraga Caespitosa. Pure white flowers from dense green tufts.

Saxifraga Decipiens. Guilford's hybrids. Lovely shades of rose and pink, foliage forms a soft evergreen carpet.

Saxifraga Macnabiana. Foliage in rosettes, silver gray to bronze in winter, flowers white with pink dots. 10 in.

Saxifraga Megasea. Cordifolia. Handsome broadleaved foliage, which alone would make them invalnable. Rose pink flowers very early in large clusters.

Saxifraga Pyramidalis. Very robust, 2 ft. when in flower. Rosettes large and glaucous, white flowers in large panicles. A fine showy plant.

Saxifraga Umbrosa. London Pride. Leaves form dense rosettes 6 in. across. Flowers white speckled carmine.

Sedum Acre. Stems creeping branched, flower stems 2-3 in. high. Flowers yellow. Thrives in poor soil.

Sedum Album. Habit same as above. Flowers white. 3-4 in. June to August.

Sedum Kamtschaticum. Branches 6-10 in. long. Flower stems 4-6 in. high, flowers numerous, yellow. June to August.

Sedum Middendorfianum. Dark serrated foliage, yellow flowers.

Sedum Purpurascens. Flowers rose colored, foliage purplish.

Sedum Sexangulare. Flowers yellow, 2-3 in. June to August.

Sedum Spectabile. One of the prettiest erect growing sedums. Broad light green foliage, with immense flat heads of rose colored flowers. 30c.

Sempervivium Arachnoideum. Cobweb Hen and Chickens. The tips of the leaves are connected with long, soft white hairs. Salmon pink flowers on 3-4 in. stems.

Sempervivium Glaucum. Rose colored flowers, foliage gray green.

Sempervivium Laggeri. Leaves gray green, red violet at the tips. Flowers rose.

Sempervivium Montanum. Flowers mauve red on 3-6 in. stems.

Sempervivium Tectorum. Rosettes 3-4 in. in diameter. Leaves tipped with red brown. Flowers rose colored.

Sempervivium Triste. Leaves brownish, flowers white.

Silene Acaulis. Cushion pink. Moss-like tufted plant 2-in. high with reddish flowers. 40c.

Silene Alpestris. White flowers. An elegant dwarf species. 40c.

Silene **Shafta.** The most satisfactory of all silenes. Trailing, 3-6 in. Carmine flowers.

Thymus Serpyllum. Thyme. Forms dense mats of dark green, fragrant foliage and clouds of white flowers.

Thymus Coccineum. A rosy red flowering form of the preceding.

Thymus Lanuginosus. Woolly Thyme. Same habit as preceding, but with woolly foliage and pink flowers. An unusually good creeper.

Tritoma **Pfitzerii.** Red Hot Poker. Rich blooming border plants. Very decorative with 3-4 ft. spikes of bloom. 35c.

Tritoma Corallina. Flowers yellow. Plant more dwarf than the preceding. 35c.

Tradescantia Virginica. Spider Wort. Good for moist places. Brilliant blue flowers 12-18 in. high. May to September.

Veronica **Cataractae.** A gem for the rockery. White flowers in profusion.

Veronica Corymbosa Stricta. A fine alpine, dense plumes of azure blue flowers.

Veronica **Prostrata.** Flowers blue, lovely trailer 3 in. high. May and June.

Veronica Spicata. Flowers violet blue in long spikes. Dwarf habit.

Veronica Spicata Alba. Flowers white.

Veronica Spicata Rosea. Very neat dwarf form. Flowers pink.

Veronica Repens. Fine trailing species with deep blue flowers.

Viola Bosniaca. Flowers rosy lilac. April-Sept. 30c.

Viola Jersey Gem. Flowers fine purple. An extremely heavy all-season bloomer. 30c.

Viola G. Wermig. Large blue flowers all summer long. 30c.

Viola Rivieriana. An excellent violet for the rockery, standing sun and drought. Flowers light blue. All summer.

Zauschneria Californica. A low-growing perennial with red fuchsia-like flowers. Remarkably drought resistant. Foliage a pleasing gray. Trailing. July to October.

MISCELLANEOUS BULBS AND ROOTS

These are only available for fall planting. In addition to the ones listed we grow a limited number of other interesting native plants from the east, middle west and south. We have also a fine collection of western wild flowers and bulbs. Correspondence solicited regarding these wildlings. Write for our paeony list.

Autumn Crocus. Colchicum Autumnale. Broad green leaves in spring, which die down in summer. Lovely orchid crocus flowers in early fall. 25c.

Blood Root. Sanguinarea Canadense. A low perennial with pure white water lily like flowers in early spring. 25c.

Black Calla of the Nile. Amorphophallus Rivieri. Flowers are like huge callas but of a dark chocolate color. Individual flowers are sometimes a foot and a half long. Tubers 35c to $1.00, according to size.

Feather Hyacinth. Lovely and curious flowers 9 inches high with feathery plume-like spikes of lovely lilac blue color. Fine for the rock garden. $1.50 a doz.

FERNS

These are native eastern and southern species for dry shady places.

Athyrium. Filix Femina. Lady Fern. A large handsome fern from one to three feet high. 35c.

Dennstedtia Punctilobula. Hay-scented Fern. 12-18 in. Will grow in sun or shade, soon forming a compact mass. 35c.

Dryopteris Clintoniana. Clinton's Wood Fern. 2 ft. or more in height, producing fine masses of greenery. 35c.

Osmunda Cinnamonea. Cinnamon Fern. 2-4 ft. high, 8 in. wide. Likes a peaty soil. 50c.

Osmunda Claytoniana. Interrupted or Flowering fern. Prefers a dry, stony soil. Thrives in the open sun. Popular for porch and foundation planting. 50c.

Osmunda Regalis. Royal fern. Pale green fronds. 2-3 ft. It can be grown in still water. A lovely fern. 50c.

Pteretis Nodulosa. Ostrich Plume Fern. Fronds 3-5 ft. by 6-10 in. wide. An erect handsome species. Graceful as a palm. Plant in leaf mold or rotted peat. 50c.

Pellaea Atropurpurea. A small rock loving fern with attractive gray green fronds and black stems. Stands drought and sun well. Native of Texas. Hardy. 35c.

LILIES

Aratum. Gold Banded Lily of Japan. Immense white flowers thickly spotted with brown, each petal having a golden yellow band through the center. 25c.

Candidum. Madonna Lily. Waxy white flowers in large clusters. June flowering. 25c.

Canadense. Canada Lily. 2-4 ft. Flowers various shades of yellow, orange and red. 35c.

Caroliniamum. Carolina Lily. Flowers orange red and very fragrant. Rare. 35c.

Elegans. Upright flowers in shades of orange and red. 35c.

Giganteum. Easter Lily. Lovely large white lily bells. 35c.

Grayi. Gray's Lily. 2-4 ft. A beautiful lily with deep reddish bell shaped flowers. Showy. 35c.

Pardalinum. Leopard Lily. Bright scarlet and yellow flowers spotted with rich brown. Robust and free flowering. 35c.

Regale. Regal Lily. A strong growing lily of easy culture. Ivory white flowers tinted with pink and brown on reverse of petals. 50c.

Speciosum. Rubrum. Flowers white with a pink band in the center of each petal, and numerous crimson spots toward the center of the flower. 30c.

Superbum. Turk's Cap Lily. 4-8 ft. Flowers bright orange with dark purple spots. A heavy bloomer, fine among shrubbery and in border plantings. 30c.

Tigrinum. Fortuni. Tiger Lily. Well known variety. Rich orange and yellow flowers marked with small black spots. Double and single varieties. 30c.

BULBS

Grape Hyacinth. California Giants. Much larger than ordinary Grape Hyacinths. Fine deep blue. Fine for the rock garden or naturalizing. 75c per doz.

Iris, English. Lovely wide petaled flowers similar to Japanese iris, foliage grass like. A very deep blue. $1.50 per doz.

Iris, Spanish. Narrow petaled flowers in a wide range of colors. Mixed shades of white, yellow, bronze, lavender and blue. $1.00 per doz.

Jack-in-the-Pulpit. Arisaemma Triphyllus. Curious black and green calla-like flowers from the Middle West. Plant in the shade. 25c.

Tigridia Pavonia. Shell Flower. Leaves sword shape, 1½-2½ ft. tall. Flowers are three petaled, cup-shaped shaded apricot salmon with maroon spots in the center of the flower. Produced in succession through the summer. $1.50 per doz.

Scilla. Nutans. Wood Hyacinth. Lovely Spring flowering bulbs with small hyacinth-like flowers in shades of white, blue and pink. Mixed shades only. 75c per doz.

AQUATICS

We grow the following aquatic plants suitable for pools.

Prices 25c except as noted.

Parrot's Feather. A dainty feathery leafed foliage plant which floats on the water.

Water Hawthorn. Oblong green leaves and sweet scented flowers, white with purple dots. Very free blooming.

Water Poppy. Heart-shaped bronzy leaves and yellow blossoms much like California poppies.

Pickerel Weed. For the edge of the pool. Big sturdy leaves rising from the water. Flowers a lovely blue. 50c.

Water Hyacinth. Round bulb-like leaves inflated with air, flowers soft blue. Goldfish spawn on the roots of this plant. Not hardy.

WATER LILIES

Nymphea Odorata. White sweet scented. Free flowering. $1.00.

Chromotella. Pale yellow flowers, leaves green mottled with brown. A heavy bloomer. $1.50.

Rosea. Soft pink. Sweet scented. $1.50.

Pink. Rose Arey. Very lovely deep rose pink. Fragrant and free blooming. One of the very best. $4.50.

Mrs. Shaw. A large flowering deep red. $3.00.

GOLDFISH

We grow a fine lot of fish of the following varieties: Common goldfish, comets, Japanese fantails, shubunkins, and telescopes. Prices 25c to $1.00, according to size.

IRIS

The iris is one of the most satisfactory plants in cultivation, thriving in almost any situation and under almost any conditions. It is tall, 4 to 5 feet; it is dwarf, 3 to 12 inches. The range of colors is wide; every tone and shade is represented except the shocking red of the salvia. The foliage is ornamental, the blooming season long. What more could any garden lover wish?

We are glad to welcome visitors at any time, even in winter, when the lovely Speciosa is in bloom. The dwarf bearded iris begin blooming early in April, and from then until July first our gardens are a veritable riot of color. We recommend a visit to our gardens during the blooming season, as we feel that a better selection can be made if the plants are seen in bloom in the field.

SPECIES OF BEARDLESS IRIS

This list contains some of the most desirable species, varieties, and hybrids.

Acoroides. Sprays of canary yellow flowers with brown veins. Very fine. A native of Syria. 50c.

Chrysographes. Yellow and blue. A fine variety. $1.00. China.

Cristata. Plant dwarf; very fine blue flowers. A good rock garden subject. 35c. Mountains of West Virginia.

Delavayi. Rich violet flowers. Native of Tibet. $1.00.

Foetidissima. The seed pods remain in the plant in winter, bursting open and displaying rows of orange red berries. The flowers are inconspicuous. Central and southern Europe. 50c.

Foresti. A dwarf yellow. $1.00.

Fontanesi. Lilac flowers. 50c.

Foliosa. A beautiful purple blue. 50c.

Fulva. Reddish brown or copper colored. Southern U. S. 50c.

Graminea. Violet blue flowers. Very fragrant. 50c.

Gracilipes. Lovely blue flowers. Fine rock garden subject. Rare. $1.50.

Hookeri. A beautiful blue iris. 50c.

Hyacinthiana. A new introduction from Kansu, China. Very ornamental. Flowers pale blue and white. 75c.

Japonica. Evergreen foliage. Lilac flowers in racemes. Frilled. Shady border. Japan and China. 50c.

Longipetala. Flowers bright lilac. 35c.

Missouriensis. Various shades of blue. S. D. to Ariz. 50c.

Prismatica. Lilac purple with yellow throat; darker veins. Eastern U. S. 50c.

Ochroleuca. White stained yellow. 50c.

Pseudoacorus. Deep yellow flowers with brown veins. Wet sunny position. S. Europe and Syria. 35c.

Ruthenica. Deep blue purple flowers. North China. $1.00.

Stylosa. Flowers deep reddish purple. Blooms November to April. Should have a place in every garden. Algeria. 50c.

Tectorum. Japanese roof iris. Violet blue frilled petals. Very large crest. A most interesting type. 50c.

Tenax. Dainty flowers in various shades of white and lavender. Heavy bloomer. Native of Cascade Mountains. 35c.

Verna. Dwarf. Very choice. Clear violet. One of the best. Shade. Kentucky and Virginia. 50c.

Versicolor. Violet blue. Northern U. S. 35c.

Wilsonii. Seedlings, yellow to purple. Western China. 75c.

SIBERICA

Emperor. Tall; a fine dark blue purple. 50c.

Lady Northcliffe. Tall. White ground with dark blue penciling. 50c.

Miss Dodo. Large flowers, blue veined white. 50c.

Perry's Blue. The best light blue. 50c.

Superba. Blue. 50c.

Snow Queen. A splendid white. Good for cutting. 50c.

True Blue. Azure blue of splendid texture. 50c.

Dorothea K. Williamson. Deep velvety purple flowers. A fine exhibition flower. 50c.

DWARF IRIS

In the descriptions "S" denotes standard or upright petals; "F" denotes falls or drooping petals.

Pumila, Chameiris and Hybrids.

Albatre. 7½-inch; a near white, veined pale lilac, beards white. 35c.

Alpin. 5-inch. S., Lobelia blue; F., reddish purple. 35c.

Armee D'Orient. S., yellow; F., lightly washed violet. 35c.

Azurea. 6-inch. Very early; sky blue. 75c.

Barbara. 10-inch. Cream, purple and olive. 35c.

Balceng Bluebeard. 10-inch. Cream, green and blue. 25c.

Balceng Curiosity. 10-inch. Yellow, purple and olive. 25c.

Balkana. 8-inch. Reddish purple. 50c.

Biflora. 6-inch. Purple violet. 35c.

Bluestone. 6-inch. S., violet; F., purple. 35c.

Boquet. 6-inch. White and pale red. 35c.

Brautjunfer. 6-inch. S., lilac white; F., yellow at base, purple at ends. 35c.

Burgos. 6-inch. Violet lilac, a reddish tone. 35c.

Buzzer. 9-inch. S., light lavender blue; F., same color, overcast rusty; gives the falls a pink tone. 75c.

Canari. 9-inch. Straw yellow self. 35c.

Candida. 6-inch. A white self. 50c.

Chameiris Aurea Maculata. 6-inch. Yellow and maroon. 35c.

Comandant Driant. 6-inch. S., white tinted violet; F., violet. 35c.

Contesse Hautville. 6-inch. S., violet purple; F., garnet. Extra good. 35c.

Cyanea. 6-inch. A medium blue self. Good 25c.

Danny Boy. 6-inch. S., Red purple; F., darker, rich red beard. $1.00.

Ditton Purple. 5-inch. This is one of my best; dark plum, purple self. 35c.

Dixmude. 6-inch. Dark blue and reddish violet. 35c.

Endymion. 9-inch. Very beautiful dark ruby red self. 50c.

a bo Lights. 8-inch. Best light sulphur yellow. 75H r r

Huron Imp. 6-inch. Very large flowers; dark blue, almost black; very floriferous. $1.00.

Judy. 9-inch. A dark ruby self; very fine. 75c.

Le Lido. 8-inch. Lilac self. 35c.

Lutea. 6-inch. Yellow self. 25c.

Marocain. 10-inch. One of the best dark blues. 50c.

Macrocarpa. 5-inch. A true pumila of rich violet tones. The very earliest to bloom. 35c.

Max. 6-inch. S., gold yellow; F., darker, a very fine iris. $1.50.

Mistral. 8-inch. S., violet purple; F., reddish purple. 35c.

Negus. 5-inch. Dark blue purple self. 35c.

Niobe. 5-inch. This is a real beauty. Very dwarf; dark purple self; blue beard. One of the best blue blacks. 35c.

Nudicaulis. 8-inch. Reddish blue. 35c.

Orange Queen. 8-inch. Deep yellow self. One of the fine dark yellows. 35c.

Oriental. 8-inch. S., ruby red; F., garnet. 75c.

Petite Amie. 8-inch. Greenish white and cream. 35c.

Reichenbachi. 6-inch. Yellow self. 35c.

Reichenbachi. 6-inch. Var. orange; deeper yellow than type. 35c.

Royal Purple. 6-inch. A very dark purple self. 35c.

Snow Cap. 10-inch. White self. 35c.

Silver Elf. 10-inch. S., pure white; F., gray, delicately lined light blue. 75c.

Socrates. 8-inch. Claret red self. A very fine dwarf. 50c.

Trautlieb. 12-inch. A very fine pink. 35c.

Wigan. 8-inch. The general tone as viewed from a distance is a brownish red. Very pretty. 50c.

Zobeida. 6-inch. S., smoky lavender; F., dark velvety lavender purple, with a bloom on the petals. 35c.

JAPANESE IRIS

These lovely iris are as yet but too little known. They bloom after the bearded iris and continue for some weeks. They do best planted in sunlight and well watered previous to blooming. Best results are obtained when they are fertilized with sheep manure. Beside the named varieties listed below we also have a number of lovely unnamed varieties of equal merit. We would be pleased to have you visit our gardens during the blooming season, as Japanese Iris need to be seen in bloom to be fully appreciated. The number of petals is designated by the figure in parenthesis.

Albatross. (6) Beautiful pure white, best of all double whites. 50c.

Aspasia. (3) Amethyst with delicate blue lines radiating from the central yellow bar. Center darker. $1.00.

Ayasi. (3) Claret; penciled white surrounding the gold bar, stamens white tipped lavender. 50c.

Avigata. (3) Dark plum and gray with purple veins. 50c.

Azure. (6) Immense flower exquisitely waved, mauve blue, darker halo surrounding yellow blotch at base of petals. 50c.

Catherine Parry. (6) Blue overlaid rosy red, high tufts in center almost triple. 50c.

Clarice Childs. (3) Petunia violet conspicuous yellow center surrounded with blue. Large. 75c.

Cloud Dress. (6) Gray ground with prominent purple lines radiating from the gold bar. 50c.

Choisei-Den. (6) Ruffled claret and white. 50c.

Columbia. (6) Blue with pure white veins. A striking variety. 50c.

Date-Dogu. (3) Rich claret red, orange blotches surrounded by blue halo. 50c.

Dominator. (3) Rich indigo blue with narrow white stripes and light center. One of the finest. 50c.

Doris Childs. (6) Pearl white deeply veined rosy plum, center petals deep plum edged white. 50c.

Sofu-No-Koi. (6) Mottled blue and gray. 50c.

Shadow. (3) Reddish purple self. Large and fine. 50c.

Shiga. (6) Reddish blue, orange bar surrounded by white with radiating white lines. A large handsome flower. 75c.

Tai-Hier-Ka. (6) A fine red. 50c.

Tora-Odori. (3) Gray overlaid lavender blue, very large and fine. $1.

T. S. Ware. (6) Reddish violet flowers veined white. 50c.

Uchiu. (6) Cerulean blue, veined white. Gold center. Exquisite. 50c.

Wase Banri. (3) White with lavender standards. 50c.

Yedo-Jiman. (3) Thunder bolt. Dark royal blue with white halo. 50c.

Zama-No-Mori. (3) White shaded azure blue, large and beautiful. $1.00.

Eleanor Parry. (6) Claret red flamed white and blue. 50c.

Fascination. (6) Blue lightly veined white with a pink tinge. 50c.

Gekko-No-Nami. (6) White with prominent yellow bar. Petals drooping. 50c.

Goko. (3) Mottled blue. Very wide petals. 50c.

Gold Bound. (6) White. 50c.

Idzumi-Gawa. (6) Gray radiating dark blue veins. 50c.

Kombarin. (6) Large early white. 50c.

Komchi-Guma. (6) Very double deep violet purple. 50c.

Kuro Kumo. (6) Deep purple overlaid with blue; purple bar. 50c.

Kyoto. (6) Very lovely orchid lavender penciled white. One of the showiest. 50c.

La Favorite. Large, fine. White freely veined blue with a rich purple center. 50c.

Lavender Giant. (3) Extremely large lavender blue. Free bloomer. $1.00.

Marjorie Parry. (6) Delicate light mauve. Extra fine. $1.00.

Minerva. (3) Pink tinted rose. 50c.

Morning Mists (Usa-Ga-Umi). (3) Pure white with faint mist of pale blue. $1.00.

Mount Hood. (6) Light blue shaded darker, bright orange center. 50c.

Olympia. (3) Large white flowers veined blue, center petals delicate mauve and blue. 50c.

Patrocle. (3) Superb dark reddish violet. 50c.

Purple and Gold. (6) Early and free blooming. 50c.

Pyramid. (6) Violet purple veined white in the center of each petal. 50c.

Red Riding Hood. (3) A fine amaranth veined and suffused white. 50c.

Reine Des Balgares. Deep blue shading with age to light blue with white veins. A fine free flowering plant. 50c.

Sano Natashi. (6) White. 50c.

TALL BEARDED IRIS

Afterglow. Grayish lavender, shading to yellow. 25c.

Alcazar. Large flowered. S., light mauve; F., cotinga purple. A most striking iris, compelling admiration by reason of its imposing stature. 50c.

Ambassadeur. S., smoky reddish violet; F., dark velvety reddish violet, one of the best of all, very striking and handsome. $1.00.

-Anna Farr. A lovely white. S., erect, cupped; F., drooping, markings at the tip of S. and base of F., light hyssop violet, prominent orange bear beard. 50c.

Anne Leslie. S., white, rose tinted; F., dahlia carmine. 50c.

Ann Page. Uniform pale blue, probably the best pale blue variety existing. $1.50.

Apricot. A soft apricot self. A charming flower of unusual coloring when fully open. 50c.

Argonaut. A clear light lavender blue. $1.00.

Aristocrat. S., lavender violet; F., dark anthacene violet with lighter edge. Flower stalk to 40 in. 25c.

Arsace. A lovely tall flower in soft lilac, with a note of gray. 25c.

Ak-Sar-Ben. Fawn and velvety brown markings on cream background. $3.00.

Asia. Soft lavender with yellow undertone. One of the grandest of all iris. $2.50.

Archeveque. Rich velvety purple bicolor. 25c.

Aurea. Rich chrome yellow. 25c.

Autocrat. Violet bicolor with attractive venation. 25c.

Avalon. A perfect iris, pinkish lavender blooms of great size and beautiful form. Fine substance. $2.00.

Azure. A very bright-toned lavender and violet bicolor. 50c.

Balboa. A tall, bright red violet bicolor. One of the Mohr giants. $2.00.

Ballerine. A handsome big fluffy flower in pale lavender with a style all its own. $1.00.

Baronet. Notable for its blue tone. Good height. 50c.

Barrelane. A large lavender violet flower of good habit. 50c.

Beau Ideal. A beautifully formed white ground plicata with petunia violet border. $1.00.

Belladona. Deep purplish blue, with S. darker than F. Early. 50c.

Benbow. S., white; F., brilliant crimson purple edged with a white line. $1.00.

Bernard Galloway. S., violet rose; F., bright rose, lined purple. A very fine flower. $1.00.

Blue Lagoon. Large flowered rich velvety deep blue. 50c.

Black Prince. S., lavender violet; F., very dark velvery violet. Unexcelled for richness of color. Late. $1.

Bluet. A useful free-flowering blue toned iris which should be much more widely planted. 50c.

B. Y. Morrison. Deep purple F., with lavender edging matching the F. 75c.

Canopus. A Dominion seedling which is an improved Alcazar. Very large flower. $2.00.

Captain Coffin. One of the bluest lavenders. Good size and pallida foliage. $1.50.

Catalosa. Violet bicolor with unusual reticulations on the falls. $1.00.

Caterina. Bluish lavender self. 25c.

Cavalier. S., clear violet; F., deep velvety blue purple. 25c.

Chalice. A bright uniform yellow self. $1.50.

Cluny. S., soft lilac blue; F., darker. 25c.

Col. Candelot. Flowers coppery red. Distinct. 50c.

Conquistator. A tall vigorous plant with fine foliage and deep mauve to light violet flowers. Size and height are outstanding. $1.50.

Corrida. Pale bluish violet self. 25c.

Crusader. Large, almost a bluish violet self Tall and distinct. 50c.

Cypriana. S., lavender violet; F., hyacinth violet. A fine variety. 25c.

Damozel. A fine ruffled plicata. 75c.

Delicatissima. Light hortense violet to pale purple self. 50c.

Dianto. S., cotinga purple; F., pansy violet. Very floriferous, as near red as any. 50c.

Dr. Bernice. S., canary bronze; F., velvety crimson. Old but very good. 25c.

Dora Longdon. S., cream buff, flushed pink at center; F., magenta to rose purple. 25c.

Dorman. A rich red purple. 25c.

Dream. A lilac self. A typical "pink" pallida. 50c.

Duke of York. One of the best of the new Perry varieties. Fine shape and texture. Flowers very large, mauve blue, with bold orange beard. $2.

Duquesne. A very rich dark blue bicolor. $1.00.

Dusky Maid. S., pale buff; F., deep mauve purple. 50c.

Eckesachs. S., lavender blue; F., purple violet. Good. 25c.

Eclaireur. S., white reflected lilac; F., rosy violet. Attractive. $1.00.

Edith Cavell. The grandest of all whites. Huge flowers with yellow throats of unusual finish and substance. $2.00.

Edouard Michel. Wonderfully ruffled dark red violet flowers. 50c.

Elberon. A new shade in a deep red. 50c.

Eldorado. A striking yellow and heliotrope blend. 25c.

Emir. A fine blue bicolor of fine height and form. 50c.

E. H. Jenkins. A very good lavender pallida. 50c.

E. L. Crandall. A heavily margined lavender and white plicata with prominent orange beard. 25c.

Eric. Pinkish lilac self. Good. 50c.

Fairy. Inexpensive, but lovely opal-tinted white plicata. 25c.

Fedora. A fine variegata. S., old gold; F., reddish violet purple. $1.00.

Flammenschwert. An improved Iris King. 50c.

Forsette. A dark lavender self. $1.00.

Fro. S., deep gold; F., brilliant chestnut brown. 50c.

Georgia. Soft shade of uniform cattleya rose. 75c.

Gertrude. A deep blue self; one of our heaviest bloomers. 25c.

Grevin. A red purple blend. 25c.

Greater May Queen. An improved May queen. 25c.

Halo. Large flowers of Lord of June type. Good substance. Light blue violet. 50c.

Harriet Presby. A very tall light rosy violet. Very free blooming. $1.50.

Her Majesty. Deeper color than May queen. 25c.

Hermoine. An immense and greatly admired light reddish purple bicolor. Late. $1.00.

Hermosa. Bright Mathews purple with a yellow glow in crests and beard. 50c.

Inca. S., saffron yellow; F., velvety dark plum, edged gold. 25c.

Ingeborg. Handsome flowered early white with yellow throat. 25c.

Iris King. A variegata with buff standards and a wide border of ox-blood red on the falls. 50c.

Isolene. Large flowers indescribably blended in pale bronze, pink-lilac and mauve. Regal when sheltered from bright sun. 35c.

Jacquesiana. A rich bronze and mahogany. 25c.

Jeanne D'Arc. An airy and very free flowered plicata. Lovely lavender penciling. 25c.

Jennett Dean. Very large flowers of pale, shimmering lavender. Exquisite when well grown. $1.50.

J. J. Dean. Brilliant blue purple. Immense flowers. Very effective. $1.00.

Jubilee. One of the best of **Mr. Sass's** interesting yellow ground plicatas. Wavy petals dotted and stippled with purple and brown. $3.00.

Juniata. A lovely, sweet-scented mauve self. 25c.

King Karl. The most perfectly formed plicata I have seen. Flowers beautifully frilled and dotted with a blend of rich colors. $3.00.

Kochii. A very early red purple self. 35c.

Koya. A deep violet self apt to bloom in the fall as well as spring. 35c.

Lady Foster. Handsome big lavender flowers. 50c.

Lady Byng. A clear pale lavender; a beautiful flower. $1.00.

La Niege. A lovely late creamy white. Still far too rare. 50c.

Lent A. Williamson. Massive in stalk and flower, deep red violet, shaded with yellow. 50c.

Leonata. An exceedingly large flower and very fragrant. A lavender flower of exceptional beauty. $2.00.

Lohengrin. A Chinese violet. Sweet scented. 25c.

Lona. Similar to King Karl, but having more lavender in the coloring. $3.00.

Lord of June. Large. S., floppy light chicory blue; F., drooping lavender violet. Handsome. 75c.

Loreli. Light yellow and purple. Floriferous and gay. 25c.

Mady Carriere. A delightful blend; in the Afterglow class. 50c.

Magnifica. Like Alcazar, but still larger also lighter and pinker. Immense blooms on tall, strong, well-branched stems. $1.00.

Ma Mie. Clear white frilled violet blue, better form than Mme. Chereau. 35c.

Marian Mohr. Pale glistening lavender. 50c.

Marsh Marigold. S., pale golden yellow; F., deep purple brown. 75c.

Mary Orth. S., light blue violet; F., dark blue violet. 50c.

Mary Garden. A yellowish plicata of considerable charm. 25c.

Mary Williamson. Purple with white bordered falls, ruffled. Distinct and interesting. $1.00.

Mauvine. Mauve, the falls a shade darker. 25c.

May Rose. Soft bright rose pink. 25c.

Medrano. General effect a dark, smoky claret. Rich and distinct. 75c.

Mesopotamica. S., lavender violet; F., hyacinth violet. $1.00.

Midguard. The best bright rose and yellow blend I have seen; a tint of ashes of roses overlays the bright color. Large flowers. $7.50.

Midwest. A dainty reddish plicata, delightfully frilled. 50c.

Minnehaha. Pale yellow with maroon reticulation. Very distinct. 35c.

Mistress Ford. A fine red purple bicolor. 75c.

Miss Wilmot. White, slightly tinted lavender. Petals of stout leathery texture. 50c.

Mlle. Schwartz. Large palest mauve self. 75c.

Mme. Boullet. Somewhat similar to Mme. Chobaut. 35c.

Mme. Chereau. A purple and white plicata. 25c.

Mme. Cheri. Ageratum violet washed with pink. One of the best. 50c.

Mme. Chobaut. Flowers of pale yellow, shaded and veined with cinnamon brown. Unusual coloring. Good. 35c.

Mme. De Sevigne. A fine large plicata, with violet purple markings. 25c.

Mme. Durrand. An indescribable tan and mauve blend. Very tall and large. $5.00.

Monsignor. S., violet; F., heavily veined a deeper purple. 25c.

Montezuma. S., deep yellow dotted brown; F., yellow and white, veined purple and dotted brown. 35c.

Mons. Hubert. A violet and blue blend. 75c.

Moonstone. Pale, soft luminous blue. 50c.

Morning Splendor. S., petunia violet; F., raisin purple. Very large flowers; producing a striking, deep red in sunlight. $4.00.

Mother of Pearl. A large flowered pale lavender iris of remarkably pearly tone. Free flowering and vigorous. 50c.

Mrs. Alan Grey. A delightful pinkish lavender, often blooms in fall. 25c.

Mrs. Chas. Pearson. A fine light mauve lavender. $1.00.

Mrs. Fryer. S., pale lavender; F., red purple. 25c.

Mrs. Tinley. Large self of violet blue. 25c.

Mrs. Walter Brewster. S., lavender blue; F., analine blue. 50c.

Myth. Light lavender, big ruffled flowers. Very good. 50c.

Nancy Orne. A tall raspberry lilac toned iris. Lovely in the garden. 50c.

Neibelungen. Olive buff and violet. 25c.

Neptune. One of the big purple bicolors. 50c.

Nue. D'Orage. A ruffled smoky lavender flower with an illuminated center. 25c.

Nimbus. S., light lobelia violet; F., cotinga purple. A very beautiful steel gray flower. $1.50.

Nine Wells. Extremely striking rich purple flower of fine height and habit. 35c.

Nothung. A combination of sulfur yellow and palest blue. 50c.

Nubian. S., mauve; F., raisin purple. 50c.

Oliver Perthuis. Rich purple, resembling Mme. Gaudichau, but later. $1.00.

Opera. A rich reddish bicolor. 50c.

Orchid. A delicately colored iris of grayish lavender. 50c.

Oriflamme. An early bloomer and great favorite. huge blue purple flowers in the utmost profusion. 50c.

Parc De Neuilly. Rich violet purple. Splendid garden effect. 25c.

Parisiana. S., thickly netted purple on white ground. F., creamy white, margin purple. 25c.

Pauline. Pleasing lilac pink shade. Fine garden effect. 25c.

Perfection. Rich light lavender to dark madder violet. One of the best bicolor iris. 25c.

Phyllis Bliss. Pale rosy lavender self; 50c.

Plumed Knight. Fine veining and powdering of pinkish lilac on white standards and falls. $2.00.

Pocahontas. White widely bordered lavender violet. One of the best frilled varieties. 25c.

Powhatan. A good red purple self. 25c.

Prairie Gold. Intensely brilliant yellow; sturdy growing and fine. $5.00.

Princess Beatrice. The finest form of Pallida Dalmatica; silvery lavender flowers of greatest substance. Floriferous and lovely. 35c.

Princess Victoria Louise. An early blooming yellow and plum combination. 25c.

Professor Seeliger. A deep wine purple, an attractive iris. 75c.

Prosper Laugier. Flowers of strongly bronzed crimson purple. 25c.

Prospero. Strikingly handsome purple violet bicolor, an exceptional iris. 50c.

Purple Lace. Deep blue purple except for the white ground beneath the lacing of the haft. $1.00.

Quaker Lady. S., smoky lavender; F., blue and old gold, center of flower and beard yellow. Of fine form and finish. 25c.

Queen. S., light blue splashed yellow; F., blue. $1.00.

Queen Caterina. A large pale lavender violet self. 25c.

Rachael Fox. Small but charming blend of old gold flushed with soft blue. 50c.

Red Cross. S., pinkish lavender; F., red. 25c.

Red Riding Hood. Unusual reddish tone. 25c.

Regan. A large handsome dark purple. 75c.

Rhein Nixie. S., white; F., pansy violet, bordered bluish white. 25c.

Ricardi Fonce. Large flowers of light and dark violet on well-branched stems. 75c.

Ring Dove. Large flowers of pale lavender violet on tall stems. 25c.

Romany. S., pale dusky yellow; F., bright red. 50c.

Romeo. A striking little yellow violet and lilac tricolor. 50c.

Rosalba. As near red as any. $1.00.

Rosado. A soft rosy pink on tall strong stems. $1.00.

Rose Dale. A strong grower of clear lavender overlaid with blue. $1.00.

Rose Madder. S., purple; F., dahlia purple. $2.50.

Roseway. Deep reddish pink. An effective garden iris. 50c.

Rubrissma. A deep reddish pink blend. 25c.

Ruby Perry. A lovely dark rose pallida. On stems of nearly four feet. $1.00.

Ruby Queen. A distinct ruby iris. 35c.

Rugago. Wine red in tone. Valuable for garden effects. 50c.

San Gabriel. Enormous lavender mauve flowers on 4-5 ft. stems. Early and long flowering. A wonderful iris. $2.00.

Santa Barbara. A fine pure lavender blue of stunning garden effect. $5.00.

Seminole. Rich red purple with velvety falls. 50c.

Shalimar. A trojana seedling of rich color. Remarkable for its numerous flowers. 25c.

Shekinah. One of the finest yellows. Soft and clear. 50c.

Sherbert. An unusual bicolor in old gold and brown. 25c.

Sherwin Wright. A small but good bright yellow. 25c.

Sindjkha. Subdued tones but of magnificent habit and growth. 25c.

Soledad. An early flowering clear, soft yellow. 50c.

Solana. S., clear yellow; F., deep red. 25c.

Souvenir De Mme. Gaudichau. Rich deep violet, magnificent both as specimen and clump. No iris lover should be without it. $1.00.

Speciosa. Lovely soft blue with a distinct ripe grape odor. 25c.

Steepway. A smooth blend of satiny texture. S., reddish fawn; F., mauve shaded with blue and brown. $1.00.

Sunset. A free flowering variety with blooms of unusual coloring. S., olive gold; F., flushed mauve at the center. Late. $1.00.

Susan Bliss. Uniform shade of deep rose pink, vigorous and free flowering. $2.50.

Suzanne Autissier. S., analine blue; F., velvety purplish violet. $1.00.

Sweet Lavender. S., French gray lavender; F., rosy lavender; distinct from all other lavender iris. $1.00.

Tamerlane. Large violet purple flowers. 35c.

Thelma Perry. Pale lliac pink. F., slightly deeper than S. Reticulated deep bronze at the base. $1.00.

Titan. Enormous flowers on tall stems. S., light violet blue; F., violet purple. The most striking iris in cultivation. $2.00.

Toreador. S., brilliant orange shot with bronze; F., rich glowing red. 25c.

Troost. S., deep rosy purple; F., paler veined violet changing to brown at top. 50c.

Trojana. A good early blue. 25c.

True Charm. White margins etched with blue lavender. Very lovely and frilled. $2.00.

Turco. Soft violet buff. A peculiar color. 25c.

Variegata. Yellow and green variegated foliage. Blue flowers. 50c.

Victorine. An interesting white and violet combination. 25c.

Violacea. S., rich blue; F., violet blue. 25c.

Virginia Moore. Very good late lemon yellow. 50c.

Western Dream. A light violet self of great beauty. 50c.

White Knight. Pure snow white. 25c.

White Queen. A pure white somewhat earlier than White Knight. Very prolific bloomer. 50c.

Yvonne Pelletier. One of the very finest of the pale blue varieties. Late. 50c.

Zouave. A dainty lilac plicata. 50c.

Zua. White with a lavender tint. Flowers heavily crimped, creped and frosted. Early. Entirely distinct from all other iris. 50c.

CPSIA information can be obtained
at www.ICGtesting.com
Printed in the USA
LVHW080808051218
599325LV00003B/248/P